QUICK GUIDE

12 Law & Tax
GUIDELINES
for New Ministers

| **RICHARD R. HAMMAR**
J.D., LL.M., CPA

Copyright © 2016 Christianity Today International.
All rights reserved.

No part of this book may be reproduced, stores in a retrieval system, or transmitted, in any form or by any means, electronic, mechanical, photocopying, recording, or otherwise, without prior written permission from the publisher, except in the case of brief quotations embodied in critical articles and reviews.

For information, contact:
    Church Law & Tax Team
    Christianity Today International
    465 Gundersen Drive
    Carol Stream, IL 60188

This publication is designed to provide accurate and authoritative information in regard to the subject matter covered. It is sold with the understanding that the publisher is not engaged in rendering legal, accounting, or other specific service. If legal advice or other expert assistance is required, the services of a competent professional person should be sought. From a Declaration of Principles jointly adopted by a Committee of the American Bar Association and a Committee of Publishers and Association.

Visit our website, *ChurchLawAndTax.com.*

Contents

Introduction 5

Chapter-1 Are You a "Minister" for Federal Tax Purposes? 7

Chapter-2 Should I Report My Income Taxes as an
Employee or as Self-Employed 17

Chapter-3 Should You Report Your Social Security
Taxes as an Employee or as Self-Employed? 25

Chapter-4 Should You "Opt Out" of Social Security? 29

Chapter-5 What Is the Housing Allowance? 39

Chapter-6 What are the Tax Consequences of Living in
a Church-Owned Parsonage? 45

Chapter-7 How Do You Pay Estimated Taxes? 51

Chapter-8 Can You Have the Church Withhold Your Taxes? 61

Chapter-9 What Is the Best Way for You to Handle
Business Expenses? 67

Chapter-10 What Is the Clergy-Penitent Privilege? 75

Chapter-11 Are You Required to Report Child Abuse? 83

Chapter-12 What Legal Requirements Apply to
the Performance of Marriage Ceremonies? 91

Resources 103

Introduction

If you're like most new ministers, you probably are overwhelmed by the legal and tax issues that confront you in the ministry. Who is a minister for federal tax purposes? Should I report my taxes as an employee or as self-employed? Should I "opt out" of Social Security? What is the housing allowance? What are the tax consequences of living in a church-owned parsonage? Do I have taxes withheld from my wages, or am I required to pay estimated taxes? What is the best way for me to handle business expenses? What is the clergy-penitent privilege? Am I required to report child abuse? What legal requirements apply to the performance of marriage ceremonies?

It is essential that you, as a new minister, be familiar with the legal requirements and tax rules that apply to your vocation. Unfortunately, few begin their ministry with this knowledge. This is usually because you received no formal training on legal or tax issues during your theological training, or because the information you received was inadequate. You are expected to acquire this information "on the job." In most cases, this simply does not happen. There must be a better way.

This book was created to provide new ministers with quick, understandable answers to the kinds of questions mentioned above. Those who want more information on any of these issues can easily find it, along with information on hundreds of other legal and tax issues, at **ChurchLawAndTax.com.**

We hope that you'll find the information presented in this book useful. We have attempted to address the most important issues, without overloading you with technical jargon, all with the hope that you'll flourish in ministry.

—Richard R. Hammar

CHAPTER 1

Are You a "Minister" for Federal Tax Purposes?

A number of federal tax laws have unique application to ministers. You should determine if you fall under the IRS's definition of a "minister" in order to properly determine and report your federal income taxes. In this chapter, you'll learn about special tax rules for ministers and whether you qualify for them.

Test your knowledge

Before we start, take a few minutes to complete the following quiz and find out how much you already know. You'll find the answer key at the end of the chapter. Don't worry if you don't know all the answers yet; you'll learn as you read the chapter.

QUIZ
Select true or false:

1. Pastor J is an ordained minister who serves as a minister of education at his church. He occasionally conducts worship services, but does not administer the sacraments. He does have management responsibility in his local church and at regional and national meetings of his denomination. His duties include

overseeing the educational program of his church, occasional counseling, and hospital visitation. Pastor J is a "minister" for federal tax purposes.

❏ True   ❏ False

2. Pastor B is minister of music at her church. She is not ordained, commissioned, or licensed. Because she is directly involved in worship services, the church can treat her as a minister for federal tax purposes.

❏ True   ❏ False

3. Pastor R is a licensed minister who serves as the youth pastor at his church. He regularly performs sacerdotal duties and conducts religious worship. He is a minister for federal tax purposes.

❏ True   ❏ False

4. Pastor G is an ordained minister who resigned his pastoral position and temporarily is working for a "secular" employer. Since he is an ordained minister, he should be treated as a minister for tax purposes by his employer. This means that income taxes should not be withheld from his wages, and he should be treated as self-employed for Social Security.

❏ True   ❏ False

5. There are several special tax rules that apply to "ministers." These include the housing allowance, self-employed status for Social Security, and exemption of wages from income tax withholding.

❏ True   ❏ False

The Main Idea

"Ministers" are eligible for the following five special tax rules with respect to services they perform in the exercise of their ministry: the housing allowance; the parsonage exclusion; exemption from Social Security coverage (if several conditions are met); self-employed status for Social Security (if not exempt); and exemption from income tax withholding. In deciding if a person is a "minister" for federal tax purposes, the following five factors must be considered:

1. the person must be ordained, commissioned, or licensed;
2. administration of sacraments;
3. conduct of religious worship;
4. management responsibilities in the local church or a parent denomination;
5. considered to be a religious leader by the church or parent denomination.

In general, the IRS and the courts require that a minister be ordained, commissioned, or licensed, and then they apply a "balancing test" with respect to the other four factors. The more of them that a person satisfies, the more likely that he or she will be deemed to be a minister for tax reporting purposes.

5 special tax rules that apply to ministers

1. Ministers who own their home do not pay federal income taxes

on the portion of their church compensation that is designated in advance by their church as a housing allowance to the extent that the allowance is used to pay for housing related expenses and does not exceed the annual rental value of the home.

2. Ministers do not pay federal income taxes on the annual rental value of a parsonage provided by their church.
3. Ministers are exempt from "self-employment taxes" (Social Security taxes paid by the self- employed) if several conditions are met.
4. Ministers' employment status for Social Security is self-employed.
5. Ministers' wages are exempt from income tax withholding.

Income tax regulations

All of the special tax rules summarized above are available only to ordained, commissioned, or licensed ministers of a church with respect to service performed in the exercise of ministry.

This critical terminology is defined in the income tax regulations as follows:

> Service performed by a minister in the exercise of his ministry includes the ministration of sacerdotal functions and the conduct of religious worship, and the control, conduct, and maintenance of religious organizations ... under the authority of a religious body constituting a church or church denomination. ... Services performed by a minister in the control, conduct, and maintenance of a religious organization relates to directing, managing, or promoting the activities of such organization.

In short, the five special rules summarized above apply to persons who satisfy two requirements: They must be a minister, and they must be engaged in the exercise of ministry.

Court rulings

The leading case defining the term "minister" is a 1989 Tax Court case, *Knight v. Commissioner, 92 T.C. 199 (1989)*. The court announced a new test for determining whether or not a particular individual is a minister. Under this test, the following five factors must be considered in deciding whether or not a person is a minister for federal tax reporting purposes: (1) does the individual administer the "sacraments," (2) does the individual conduct worship services, (3) does the individual perform services in the "control, conduct, or maintenance of a religious organization" under the authority of a church or religious denomination, (4) is the individual "ordained, commissioned, or licensed," and (5) is the individual considered to be a spiritual leader by his or her religious body? Only the fourth factor is required in all cases (the individual must be ordained, commissioned, or licensed). The remaining four factors need not all be present for a person to be considered a minister for tax purposes. The court did not say how many of the remaining four factors must be met. It merely observed that "failure to meet one or more of these factors must be weighed ... in each case." The court concluded that the taxpayer in question was a minister despite the fact that he only satisfied three of the five factors.

It may reasonably be assumed, however, that persons who claim to be "ministers" solely on the basis of the final three factors mentioned in the Knight case will not be deemed ministers by the IRS or the courts unless they can demonstrate that they are entitled to ministerial status on the basis of other considerations. After all, if a church is willing to ordain, commission, or license its bookkeeper and secretary, these persons could argue that they satisfy the final three factors in the Knight case (management responsibilities, ordination, and a "religious leader"). The IRS and the courts will doubtless reject such a conclusion. Considerations that suggest ministerial status, even if the first two Knight factors are not satisfied, would include (1) ordaining, commissioning, or licensing to the pastoral ministry, and actual pastoral experience in the past, and (2) formal theological training.

IRS audit guidelines for ministers

In 2009 the IRS released its revised audit guidelines for its agents to follow when auditing ministers. The guidelines cover a range of issues, including the definition of the term "minister" for federal tax purposes. The guidelines provide IRS agents with the following assistance in defining the critical term "minister":

- The income tax regulations require that an individual be a "duly ordained, commissioned, or licensed minister of a church."

- The Tax Court, in *Salkov v. Commissioner, 46 T.C. 190 (1966)*, ruled that the phrase "duly ordained, commissioned, or licensed minister of a church" must be interpreted "disjunctively." By this it meant that a person qualifies as a minister for tax purposes if he or she meets any of these three categories. Ordained status, therefore, is not required.

- The guidelines add that "[t]he duties performed by the individual are also important to the initial determination whether he or she is a duly ordained, commissioned, or licensed minister.

Because religious disciplines vary in their formal procedures for these designations, whether an individual is duly ordained, commissioned, or licensed depends on these facts and circumstances."

- The guidelines, in commenting on the Knight case, note:
  The petitioner argued that he was not formally ordained as a minister and could not administer church sacraments or participate in church government. Thus, he could not be a minister subject to [self-employment taxes]. The court rejected this view, and looked at all the facts. In concluding that he was a licensed minister, it cited the facts that he was licensed by the church, he conducted worship services, and he was considered by the church to be a spiritual leader.

- The guidelines also review a 1968 Tax Court case:
  A "minister of education" in a Baptist church was not a "duly ordained, commissioned, or licensed" minister for purposes of [eligibility for a housing allowance]. The petitioner held a Master's Degree in Religious Education from a Baptist Theological Seminary, but was not ordained. Although his church "commissioned" him after he assumed the position, the court interpreted the commissioning to be for tax purposes, as it did not result in any change in duties. Most significant, however, was the court's analysis of petitioner's duties or rather, the duties he did not perform. He

did not officiate at Baptisms or the Lord's Supper, two Ordinances that closely resembled sacraments, nor did he preside over or preach at worship services. The court concluded that the evidence did not establish that the prescribed duties of a minister of education were equivalent to the duties of a Baptist minister. *Lawrence v. Commissioner, 50 T.C. 494 (1968).*

Other considerations

In deciding if a person is a minister for federal tax purposes, there are two additional points to consider:

1. **Ordained, licensed, or commissioned by one's employing church.** Many churches have a long tradition of ordaining, licensing, or commissioning ministers. But in other cases, a local church only recently has ordained, licensed, or commissioned a minister for the first time, usually to qualify the person for a housing allowance. It is far from certain that the IRS would recognize this person as a minister for tax purposes, especially if (1) the charter or bylaws of the church do not specifically authorize such a practice; (2) the person has no formal theological training; (3) the church is affiliated with a denomination that ordains, licenses, or commissions ministers, and the denomination does not recognize the ministerial status of persons who are credentialed by local congregations; or (4) the person's duties are not changed after being ordained, licensed, or commissioned. The Lawrence case (summarized above) should be reviewed in this context.

2. **"Better off" for tax purposes.** It is not necessarily true that

a church worker will be "better off" for tax purposes by becoming a minister. In many cases, a person actually will pay more taxes after being ordained, licensed, or commissioned. By becoming a minister, one will have the "benefit" of a housing allowance exclusion in computing his federal income taxes. On the other hand, the Social Security tax rate increases from 7.65 percent (the employee's share of FICA taxes) to 15.3 percent (the self-employment tax). In other words, whether or not he or she will be "better off" for tax purposes depends on whether the housing allowance exclusion offsets the additional Social Security taxes. As a result, church workers should not assume that they automatically will be "better off" for tax purposes if their church ordains, commissions, or licenses them. In many cases, they will not be.

QUIZ ANSWER KEY
1- True, 2-False, 3-True, 4-False, 5-True

CHAPTER 2

Should I Report My Income Taxes as an Employee or as Self-Employed

The issue of employment status for federal income tax purposes is important for anyone just beginning his or her ministry. This chapter will help you understand how to report your income taxes.

Test your knowledge

Before we start, take a few minutes to complete the following quiz and find out how much you already know. You'll find the answer key at the end of the chapter. Don't worry if you don't know all the answers yet; you'll learn as you read the chapter.

QUIZ
Select true or false:

1. Pastor B is an ordained minister who is currently employed as a church custodian. Since Pastor B is a minister, the church treasurer does not withhold federal income taxes from his wages. The church treasurer is correct in concluding that Pastor B's wages are not subject to income tax withholding.
   ❏ True   ❏ False

2. Wages paid to a minister for services performed in the exercise of ministry are not subject to federal income tax withholding.
   ❏ True   ❏ False

3. Pastor C is senior pastor of his church. He reports his federal income taxes as an employee. He requests voluntary withholding of his income taxes. The church treasurer assumes that if he withholds income taxes from Pastor C's wages, he is required to withhold Social Security and Medicare taxes. Is the church treasurer correct?
   ❏ True   ❏ False

4. Pastors who report their federal income taxes as employees and who request voluntary withholding may have an additional amount of income taxes withheld to cover their self-employment tax liability for the year.
   ❏ True   ❏ False

> **The Main Idea**
>
> Most new ministers should report their federal income taxes as employees, because they will be considered employees under the tests currently used by the IRS and the courts. Most clergy will be "better off" reporting as employees, since (1) the value of various fringe benefits will be excludable, (2) the risk of an IRS audit is substantially lower, and (3) reporting as an employee avoids the additional taxes and penalties that often apply to self-employed clergy who are audited by the IRS and reclassified as employees.

What difference does it make how you report your income tax?

There are two ways for a minister to report federal income taxes—as an employee or as a self-employed person.

The question of whether ministers should report their federal income taxes as an employee or as a self-employed is a significant question for many reasons, including the following:

1. **Reporting compensation.** Employees report their compensation directly on Form 1040 (line 7—wages). Self-employed persons report compensation and business expenses on Schedule C.

2. **Adjusted gross income.** Adjusted gross income is higher for ministers who report their income taxes as employees if they have unreimbursed or "nonaccountable" reimbursed business expenses since these expenses are "page two" or "below the line" deductions that are claimed after adjusted gross income is computed. Self-employed persons deduct business expenses in computing adjusted gross income. Adjusted gross income is a figure that is important for many reasons. For example, the percentage limitations applicable to charitable contributions and medical expense deductions are tied to adjusted gross income.

3. **W-2 or 1099?** Ministers working for a church or church agency should receive a Form W-2 each year if they are employees, and a Form 1099-MISC if they are self-employed (and receive at least $600 in compensation).

4. **Tax treatment of various fringe benefits.** Certain fringe

benefits provided by a church on behalf of a minister are excludable from the minister's income only if he or she is an employee. Examples include group medical insurance premiums paid by a church on behalf of its minister; group term life insurance (up to $50,000) provided by a church on behalf of a minister; amounts payable to employees on account of sickness, accident, or disability pursuant to an employer-financed plan; and employer-sponsored "cafeteria plans" which permit employees to choose between receiving cash payments or a variety of fringe benefits.

5. Audit risk. Self-employed persons face a much higher risk of having their tax returns audited. Why? IRS data reveals that the "voluntary reporting percentage" (i.e., persons who voluntarily report the correct amount of income) is much higher for employees.

6. Consequences of being reclassified as an employee. Ministers who report their federal income taxes as self-employed face a significant risk of additional taxes and penalties if they are audited by the IRS and reclassified as employees. This is because many ministers who report as self-employed deduct their unreimbursed (and "nonaccountable" reimbursed) business expenses as a deduction on Schedule C. If they are reclassified by the IRS as employees, their business expense deduction will be allowable only as an itemized deduction on Schedule A, and then only to the extent that the expenses exceed 2 percent of adjusted gross income. Ministers who are not able to itemize end up with no deduction for their business expenses. This can result in a substantial increase in taxable income.

Should I Report My Income Taxes as an Employee or as Self-Employed

The primary disadvantage of employee status is that most business expenses are deductible only as itemized deductions on Schedule A (i.e., the minister must be able to itemize deductions in order to deduct them), and they are deductible only to the extent that they exceed 2 percent of adjusted gross income. But, this "disadvantage" can be overcome simply by having your employing church adopt an accountable reimbursement policy. Under such a policy, the church reimburses you for business expenses that you periodically verify.

Employee or Self-Employed—What Difference Does it Make?

Issue	If an employee	If self-employed	How to decide if a worker is an employee or self-employed
Social Security	• employer and employee each pay FICA tax of 7.65% of employee wages (total tax of 15.3%) • ministers are never employees with regard to their ministerial duties (they do not pay FICA taxes) • nonminister church workers who are employees for income taxes are employees for Social Security (unless church filed a timely waiver from FICA taxes—in which case they are treated as selfemployed for Social Security)	• pay 15.3% self-employment tax • use Schedule SE (Form 1040) • ministers always are self-employed with regard to their ministerial duties • nonminister church workers who are selfemployed for income taxes are self-employed for Social Security	use income tax tests

income taxes	• wages reported by employer on W-2 • wages reported by worker on line 7 (Form 1040) • unreimbursed and non-accountable reimbursed expenses are deducted on Schedule A (subject to 2% floor) • low audit risk • some fringe benefits (such as employer paid medical insurance premiums and cafeteria plans) tax-free	• income reported by employer on 1099 • wages reported by worker on Schedule C and line 12 (Form 1040) • unreimbursed and nonaccountable reimbursed expenses are deducted on Schedule C • higher audit risk • some fringe benefits (such as employer paid medical insurance premiums and cafeteria plans) are taxable • church issues 1099 (if annual compensation is $600 or more)	IRS applies a 20 factor test, the Tax Court has adopted various tests; all focus on the degree of "control" exercised by the employer over the details of how the worker performs his or her job

Employee or self-employed?

The IRS and the courts have applied a bewildering number of tests to determine whether a minister is an employee or self-employed for federal income tax reporting purposes. However, three simple rules will resolve most cases:

- Senior ministers employed by a multi-staff church will almost always be treated as employees by the IRS for federal income tax reporting purposes.

- Associate ministers (e.g., youth, music) will almost always be treated as employees by the IRS for federal income tax reporting purposes.
- Senior ministers who are the only paid worker at smaller churches may be self-employed for federal income tax reporting purposes depending on the level of control exercised by the church board or congregation over how they perform their duties.

QUIZ ANSWER KEY
1- False, 2-True, 3-False, 4-True

CHAPTER 3

Should You Report Your Social Security Taxes as an Employee or as Self-Employed?

You may be surprised to learn that your employment status for income tax purposes has no bearing on your employment status for Social Security taxes. This creates some confusion for ministers, but this chapter will help you understand your employment status.

Test your knowledge

Before we start, take a few minutes to complete the following quiz and find out how much you already know. You'll find the answer key at the end of the chapter. Don't worry if you don't know all the answers yet; you'll learn as you read the chapter.

QUIZ
Select true or false:

1. A church treasurer assumes that he should treat his pastor as an employee for Social Security because the pastor is treated as an employee for income taxes. As a result, the treasurer withholds the employee's share of Social Security and Medicare taxes, and pays the employer's share as well. The treasurer has

correctly reported the pastor's Social Security taxes.
❏ True ❏ False

2. Ministers always are treated as self-employed persons under Social Security.
❏ True ❏ False

3. Pastor D is a youth pastor. To supplement his income, he also is employed part-time by a secular employer in his community. Pastor D informs the secular employer that he must be treated as self-employed for Social Security since he is a minister. Pastor D is correct. As a minister, he must be treated as self-employed for Social Security even with respect to secular employment.
❏ True ❏ False

4. Ministers compute and report their Social Security taxes on Schedule SE of Form 1040.
❏ True ❏ False

The Main Idea

Ministers are always self-employed for Social Security with respect to their ministerial services. This is true even if you are treated as an employee for federal income tax purposes. This means you pay the self-employment tax, not "Social Security" and "Medicare" taxes. Your employing church must not treat you as an employee for Social Security, even though it issues you a W-2 Form for income taxes.

One rule that never changes

There is one provision in the tax code that has caused more confusion for ministers and church treasurers than any other, and it is this: Ministers are always treated as self-employed for Social Security with regard to services they perform in the exercise of their ministry. This is true even if they are employees for federal income tax reporting. This is sometimes referred to as the "dual tax status" of ministers.

What difference does it make that ministers are always self-employed for Social Security with respect to services they perform in the exercise of their ministry? The most important consequence is that they pay the so-called "self-employment tax." This is the Social Security tax that is paid by self-employed workers. It amounts to 15.3 percent of a minister's taxable earnings. Employees and employers pay "Social Security" and "Medicare" taxes (sometimes collectively referred to as "FICA" taxes). Like self-employment taxes, these taxes amount to 15.3 percent of a minister's taxable earnings. But there is a big difference. Employers and employees split the 15.3 percent tax rate, with each paying 7.65 percent. Self-employed persons pay the entire self-employment tax. Many churches pay half, or even all, of a minister's self-employment tax. This is perfectly appropriate, but any amount paid by the church must be reported as taxable income to the minister.

Many churches withhold the employee's share of Social Security and Medicare taxes from ministers' compensation, and then pay the employer's share. In other words, they treat their minister as an employee for Social Security. This is understandable, especially when the church treats the minister as an employee for purposes of federal income taxation. But, it is always incorrect for a church to treat a minister as an employee for Social Security.

NOTE

As a self-employed person for Social Security, a minister computes self-employment taxes on Schedule SE of Form 1040.

Why are ministers treated as self-employed for Social Security?

In explaining the reason for treating ministers as self-employed for Social Security purposes, the Tax Court has observed: "Congress chose not to place the onus of participation in the old-age and survivors insurance program upon the churches, but to permit ministers to be covered on an individual election basis, as self-employed, whether, in fact, they were employees or actually self-employed." In other words, if ministers were treated as employees for Social Security purposes, then their employing churches would be required to pay the employer's share of the Social Security and Medicare tax, and this apparently was viewed as inappropriate. Of course, this justification ceased to be valid in 1984 when church employees became covered under Social Security. As a result, there is no longer any justification for the requirement that ministers are treated as self-employed for Social Security.

QUIZ ANSWER KEY
1- False, 2-True, 3-False, 4-True

CHAPTER 4

Should You "Opt Out" of Social Security?

Opting out of Social Security is an option for ministers, but you need to understand the rules and implications before making a decision. This chapter will explain the qualifications for exemption from Social Security, how to become exempt, and the consequences of opting out of the program.

Test your knowledge

Before we start, take a few minutes to complete the following quiz and find out how much you already know. You'll find the answer key at the end of the chapter. Don't worry if you don't know all the answers yet; you'll learn as you read the chapter.

QUIZ
Select true or false:

1. Pastor T's income tax return for last year (which was for the entire calendar year) showed a tax of $7,000. Pastor T projects that the tax to be shown on her current year's return will be $7,500. She also anticipates that no taxes will be withheld from her year income as a minister this year (her only source of in-

come). Pastor T is exempt from Social Security taxes. Pastor T is not required to pay estimated taxes.

❏ True   ❏ False

2. Same facts as question 1 except that Pastor T has entered into a voluntary withholding agreement with her church, and estimates that $6,500 will be withheld from her compensation this year. Pastor T is not required to pay estimated taxes.

❏ True   ❏ False

3. Pastor H is senior minister at his church. The church board fails to designate a housing allowance until May of this year. Pastor H's April 15th estimated tax payment was based on his annual earnings less an anticipated housing allowance exclusion. The delayed designation of a housing allowance will almost certainly affect Pastor H's estimated taxes for the year, and so he should recompute the remaining three quarterly payments so that an underpayment penalty is avoided.

❏ True   ❏ False

4. Pastor J does not elect voluntary withholding of any taxes, and does not use the estimated tax procedure. Instead, he simply computes his taxes for the year and sends in a check with his Form 1040. As long as Pastor J sends in a check for the full amount of his taxes, he will not be assessed an underpayment penalty as a result of his failure to comply with the estimated tax procedure.

❏ True   ❏ False

> **The Main Idea**
>
> The coverage of ministers under Social Security has caused much confusion because of two special rules. First, ministers always are self-employed for Social Security with respect to their ministerial services. This means they pay the self-employment tax, not "Social Security" and "Medicare" taxes. Second, under very limited circumstances, ministers can exempt themselves from self-employment taxes with respect to services they perform in the exercise of ministry by filing a timely Form 4361 with the IRS. The treatment of ministers under Social Security is the subject of this lesson. We will give special attention to the issue of opting out of Social Security.

What to know about Social Security

Ministers are treated very differently than other workers for Social Security purposes—they are always self-employed with respect to their ministerial services, and they pay the self-employment tax, not "Social Security" and "Medicare" taxes. Ministers are automatically covered under the Social Security system, but they are permitted to exempt themselves from coverage if they meet the following conditions:

1. Minister. Only ministers who are ordained, commissioned, or licensed by a tax-exempt church or religious organization qualify for exemption.

2. File Form 4361. The exemption application (Form 4361) must be filed on time with the IRS. The deadline is the due date of the federal tax return for the second year in which a minister has net earnings from self-employment of $400 or more, any part of which derives from the performance of services in the exercise of ministry. In most cases, this means the form is due by April 15 of the third year of ministry.

A minister certifies on Form 4361 that "I am conscientiously opposed to, or because of my religious principles I am opposed to, the acceptance (for services I performed as a minister . . .) of any public insurance that makes payments in the event of death, disability, old age, or retirement, or that makes payments toward the cost of, or provides services for, medical care." The form states that "public insurance includes insurance systems established by the Social Security Act." There are three important factors to note that new ministers often do not fully understand:

1. The tax regulations make it clear that "conscientious opposition" refers solely to religious opposition. Non-religious conscientious opposition to receiving public insurance benefits (including Social Security) does not qualify.

2. The exemption is available only if a minister is opposed on the basis of religious considerations to *the acceptance of Social Security benefits* rather than to payment of the tax. A minister may have religious opposition to payment of the tax, but this alone will not suffice. The individual must have religious opposition to *accepting* Social Security benefits upon his or her retirement or disability.

3. Participation in private insurance programs is permitted, since these are not "public insurance." As a result, a minister who files the exemption application may still purchase life insurance or participate in retirement programs administered by non-governmental institutions (such as a life insurance company or pension board).

3. Notification of ordaining, commissioning, or licensing church or denomination. Applicants for exemption must inform their "ordaining, commissioning, or licensing body" that they are opposed to Social Security coverage for services they perform in the exercise of ministry. By signing Form 4361, applicants verify that they have satisfied this requirement. Ministers who plan to apply for exemption from Social Security coverage must be sure to notify the church or denomination that ordained, commissioned, or licensed them regarding their opposition to Social Security coverage and presumably of their intention to file an exemption application. This notification must occur prior to the time the exemption application is filed.

4. IRS verification. No application for exemption will be approved unless the IRS "has verified that the individual applying for the exemption is aware of the grounds on which the individual may receive an exemption . . . and that the individual seeks an exemption on such grounds." This "verification" requirement was adopted to prevent the widespread practice of ministers exempting themselves from Social Security coverage solely on the basis of financial considerations. To satisfy this requirement, ministers must sign and return a statement the IRS mails to them to certify that they are requesting an exemption based on the grounds listed on the statement.

Common questions

Some common questions pertaining to the exemption from self-employment taxes are addressed below:

When is an exemption effective?

Filing a timely exemption application does not necessarily qualify a minister for exemption. An exemption is effective only when an applicant receives back one of the three 4361 forms (it is filed in triplicate) from the IRS marked "approved." Ministers should be careful not to lose an approved Form 4361.

Will I receive a refund of self-employment taxes I paid before filing Form 4361?

Yes. To illustrate, ministers who wait until close to the deadline for filing an exemption application will have paid self-employment taxes on their ministerial income for two years. IRS Publication 517 contains the following instructions for claiming a refund of these taxes:

> If, after receiving an approved Form 4361, you find that you overpaid SE tax, you can file a claim for refund on Form 1040X before the period of limitations ends. This is generally within three years from the date you filed the return or within two years from the date you paid the tax, whichever is later. A return you filed, or tax you paid, before the due date is considered to have been filed or paid on the due date. If you file a claim after the three-year period but within two years from the time you paid

the tax, the credit or refund will not be more than the tax you paid within the two years immediately before you file the claim.

Can the period for filing an exemption application be extended or renewed?

No. The fact that you did not acquire an opposition to Social Security until years after you became a minister will not "restart" or delay the filing deadline. One court did allow a minister to requalify for an exemption who met the following conditions: (1) change of church affiliation; (2) reordained by his new church; (3) developed an opposition, based on his new religious convictions, to the acceptance of Social Security benefits; and (4) submitted an exemption application (Form 4361) by the due date of the federal tax return for the second year in which he had net self-employment earnings of $400 or more, any part of which comes from the performance of ministerial services in his new faith.

Is an exemption from Social Security coverage irrevocable?

Yes. However, Congress has provided a few limited opportunities over the past several years for exempt ministers to revoke an exemption.

Can ministers who have opted out of Social Security receive retirement and Medicare benefits based on the fully insured status of their spouse?

Yes, according to the Social Security Administration. To the extent that a minister's spouse is fully insured under Social Security as a result of nonministerial services, Social Security benefits the minister receives as a result of his or her spouse's Social Security coverage are not based on services performed in the exercise of ministry and so are not precluded by the minister's exemption. However, the minister's benefits will be reduced by the so-called "windfall elimination provision." Under this provision, the Social Security Administration can reduce the benefits of persons who did not pay Social Security taxes, such as exempt ministers seeking benefits on the basis of their spouse's coverage. For more information on this important limitation, contact your nearest Social Security Administration office.

Can ministers who have opted out of Social Security purchase Medicare insurance after they reach age 65?

Yes.

What benefits are provided under the Social Security program?

The basic benefits are retirement benefits, disability benefits, survivor benefits, and Medicare. Note that retirement benefits, disability benefits, and survivor benefits are inflation adjusted each year, and are tax-free for most taxpayers. These benefits are available to persons who have at least 40 quarters of covered work.

Will I lose Social Security benefits based on secular employment?

Many ministers have paid Social Security taxes as a result of secular employment. If they exempt themselves from Social Security by filing a timely Form 4361, will they lose all benefits that would have been paid as a result of their secular employment? The answer is no. An exemption from Social Security only applies to services per formed in the exercise of ministry, and so exempt ministers will receive benefits based on their secular employment (assuming that they otherwise qualify). In most cases, eligibility for benefits requires at least forty quarters of coverage.

QUIZ ANSWER KEY
1- False, 2-False, 3-True, 4-False

CHAPTER 5

What Is the Housing Allowance?

Ministers who own or rent their homes, instead of living in a church-owned parsonage, are eligible for the housing allowance. In this chapter, you'll learn what a housing allowance entails, how to claim an exclusion, and more.

Test your knowledge

Before we start, take a few minutes to complete the following quiz and find out how much you already know. You'll find the answer key at the end of the chapter. Don't worry if you don't know all the answers yet; you'll learn as you read the chapter.

QUIZ
Select true or false:

1. The annual rental value of a church owned parsonage that is provided rent-free to a minister is not treated as taxable income for income tax reporting purposes.
   ❏ True   ❏ False

2. The annual rental value of a church-owned parsonage that is provided rent-free to a minister is not treated as taxable income in computing the minister's self-employment taxes.
   ❏ True   ❏ False

3. A minister lives in a church-provided parsonage. The church can designate a portion of the minister's salary as a "parsonage allowance," and this amount is not subject to income taxes if it is used to pay for parsonage-related expenses such as utilities and furnishings.
   ❏ True   ❏ False

4. A minister lives in a church-provided parsonage. The church can designate a portion of the minister's salary as a "parsonage allowance," and this amount is not subject to self-employment taxes if it is used to pay for parsonage-related expenses such as utilities and furnishings.
   ❏ True   ❏ False

5. A minister purchases a home and moves out of the church parsonage. The church lets its full-time youth minister occupy the parsonage. The youth pastor is an ordained minister. The annual rental value of the parsonage is not reported as income on the youth minster's W-2.
   ❏ True   ❏ False

6. A minister purchases a home and moves out of the church parsonage. The church lets a custodian occupy the parsonage. The annual rental value of the parsonage is not reported as income on the custodian's W-2.
   ❏ True   ❏ False

The Main Idea

Ministers who own or rent their homes can exclude from their federal income taxes the portion of their ministerial income designated by their employer as a "housing" allowance to the extent that the allowance is in fact used to pay for housing-related expenses (such as mortgage payments, utilities, property taxes and insurance, furnishings, and repairs) and does not exceed the annual "fair rental value" of their home.

How to handle a housing allowance

While a small percentage of ministers live in a manse or a church-owned parsonage, most live in a home that they own or rent. Ministers who own or rent their home do not pay income taxes on the portion of their compensation that is designated in advance by their employing church as a housing allowance—to the extent that the allowance is used to pay for housing-related expenses and, in the case of ministers who own their home, does not exceed the annual fair rental value of the home (furnished, plus utilities). There are a number of points that ministers should know about housing allowances.

1. Minister. A housing allowance is a tax-free fringe benefit (in computing income taxes) only if it is provided to a "minister of the gospel" as compensation for services performed in the exercise of ministry. Some churches designate housing allowances for nonminister church employees. This accomplishes nothing since the full amount of the allowance must be reported as taxable income to the employee.

2. An exclusion. A housing allowance is an exclusion from gross income, rather than a deduction. As a result, it is not reported anywhere on Form 1040. In effect, the exclusion is "claimed" by not reporting the allowance as income.

3. Designating a housing allowance. Whether a minister owns or rents a home, it is essential that his or her employing church designate a housing allowance. Housing allowances should be (1) adopted by the church board or congregation, (2) recorded in written form (such as minutes), and (3) designated in advance of the calendar year. However, churches that fail to designate an allowance in advance of a calendar year should do so as soon as possible in the new year. The allowance will operate starting at the time it is made.

The income tax regulations specify that the designation of the allowance may be contained in "an employment contract, in minutes of or in a resolution by a church or other qualified organization or in its budget, or in any other appropriate instrument evidencing such official action."

NOTE

Under no circumstances can a minister exclude any portion of an allowance retroactively designated by a church.

4. Amending a housing allowance. While neither the IRS nor the courts have addressed this question, it seems perfectly reasonable to conclude that a church can amend a housing allowance designation during the course of the year if changed circumstances render the allowance inadequate. Of course, any change would only operate after the time it was made.

5. How much should a church designate as a housing allowance? There is no "limit" on the amount of a minister's compensation that can be designated by a church as a housing allowance (assuming that the minister's compensation is reasonable in amount). However, for ministers who own their home, a church ordinarily should not designate a housing allowance significantly above a minister's housing expenses, or the annual fair rental value of the minister's home, since the minister can exclude the housing allowance only to the extent that it does not exceed either of these limits.

6. "Safety net" allowances. It is wise not to limit a housing allowance to a particular calendar year. For example, if a church intends to designate $10,000 of a pastor's salary as a housing allowance for the next year, its designation should recite that it is effective for the next year and all future years unless otherwise provided. This clause will protect the pastor in the event that the church neglects to designate an allowance prior to the beginning of a future year. It is also wise for a church to have a safety net designation to cover mid-year changes in personnel, delayed designations, and other unexpected contingencies. Such a designation could simply recite that "40 percent [or some other amount] of the salary of every minister on staff, regardless of when hired, is hereby designated as a housing allowance for the current year and all future years, unless otherwise specifically provided." Such "safety net" designations should not be used as a substitute for annual housing allowance designations for each minister. They are simply a means of protecting ministers against inadvertent failures by the church board to designate a timely housing allowance.

7. "Double deduction." Ministers who own their homes and who itemize their deductions are eligible to deduct mortgage interest and property taxes on Schedule A (Form 1040) even though these items were excluded as part of the housing allowance. This is the so-called "double deduction."

8. Social Security. The housing allowance is an exclusion for federal income tax purposes only. It cannot under any circumstances be excluded in computing a minister's Social Security (self-employment) tax liability. Therefore, in computing the self-employment taxes on Schedule SE (Form 1040), a minister must include the actual housing allowance exclusion as income.

QUIZ ANSWER KEY
1- True, 2-False, 3-True, 4-False, 5-True, 6-False

CHAPTER 6

What are the Tax Consequences of Living in a Church-Owned Parsonage?

Ministers who live in church-owned parsonages follow slightly different tax rules than ministers who own or rent their homes. If you live in a parsonage, you should be aware of several tax issues related to your housing situation. Read this chapter to learn what a parsonage allowance is and how to exclude it from your taxes.

Test your knowledge

Before we start, take a few minutes to complete the following quiz and find out how much you already know. You'll find the answer key at the end of the chapter. Don't worry if you don't know all the answers yet; you'll learn as you read the chapter.

QUIZ
Select true or false:

1. The annual rental value of a church-owned parsonage that is provided rent-free to a minister is not treated as taxable income for income tax reporting purposes.
   ❏ True ❏ False

2. The annual rental value of a church-owned parsonage that is provided rent-free to a minister is not treated as taxable income in computing the minister's self-employment taxes.
   ❑ True   ❑ False

3. A minister lives in a church-provided parsonage. The church can designate a portion of the minister's salary as a "parsonage allowance," and this amount is not subject to income taxes if it is used to pay for parsonage-related expenses such as utilities and furnishings.
   ❑ True   ❑ False

4. A minister lives in a church-provided parsonage. The church can designate a portion of the minister's salary as a "parsonage allowance," and this amount is not subject to self-employment taxes if it is used to pay for parsonage-related expenses such as utilities and furnishings.
   ❑ True   ❑ False

5. A minister purchases a home and moves out of the church parsonage. The church lets its full-time youth minister occupy the parsonage. The youth minster is an ordained minister. The annual rental value of the parsonage is not reported as income on the youth minister's W-2.
   ❑ True   ❑ False

6. A minister purchases a home and moves out of the church parsonage. The church lets a custodian occupy the parsonage. The annual rental value of the parsonage is not reported as income

on the custodian's W-2.
❏ True ❏ False

> **The Main Idea**
>
> Ministers can exclude from their federal income taxes the annual rental value of a parsonage provided to them as compensation for ministerial services. The annual rental value of the parsonage is not "deducted" from the minister's income. Rather, it is not reported as additional income (as it generally would be by non-clergy employees). In addition, ministers who live in a parsonage can exclude from their federal income taxes the portion of their ministerial compensation designated by their employer as a "parsonage allowance"—to the extent that it is used to pay for parsonage-related expenses such as utilities, repairs, and furnishings.

Deductions for rental value

Based on our biannual *Compensation Handbook for Church Staff* research, about 15 percent of pastors live in a church-provided parsonage or manse. This percentage declines for other ministerial staff positions. The annual fair rental value of a parsonage that is provided rent-free to a minister as compensation for ministerial services is a nontaxable fringe benefit in computing federal income taxes. The annual rental value of the parsonage is not "deducted" from the minister's income. Rather, it is not reported as additional income, as it generally would be by non-minister employees. There are a number of points that ministers should note about parsonages:

1. Minister. The annual rental value of a parsonage is a tax-free fringe benefit (in computing income taxes) only if the parsonage is provided to a "minister of the gospel" as compensation for services performed in the exercise of ministry. If a parsonage is occupied rent-free by a nonminister church employee, or a minister who is not (and never has been) an employee of the church, the annual rental value of the parsonage must be reported as taxable income.

2. An exclusion. The annual rental value of a church-provided parsonage is an exclusion from gross income, rather than a deduction. As a result, it is not reported anywhere on Form 1040. In effect, the exclusion is "claimed" by not reporting the parsonage's annual rental value as income. Many ministers find this confusing, and think that they are not receiving a tax "benefit" unless they can "deduct" something on their tax return. In fact, some ministers erroneously "deduct" the annual rental value of a parsonage in computing their taxes. This practice should be avoided.

3. Parsonage allowances. Ministers who live in a church-provided parsonage often incur expenses in "maintaining" the parsonage. Common examples include utilities, repairs, insurance, and furnishings. The portion of a minister's compensation that is designated in advance by the church as a "parsonage allowance" is nontaxable for income tax reporting purposes to the extent it is used to pay for parsonage-related expenses. The income tax regulations specify that the designation of the allowance may be contained in "an employment contract, in minutes of or in a resolution by a church or other qualified organization or in its budget, or in any other appropriate instrument evidencing such official action." The regulations further provide that "the designation ... is a sufficient designation if

What are the Tax Consequences of Living in a Church-Owned Parsonage?

it permits a payment or a part thereof to be identified as a payment of rental allowance as distinguished from salary or other remuneration." In other words, the designation must simply distinguish a part of the minister's compensation as a parsonage allowance.

A parsonage allowance should be designated by the same body (a board, or the membership) that approves compensation. A parsonage allowance must be designated in advance, since it is nontaxable only to the extent that it is used to pay parsonage-related expenses. Ideally, a parsonage allowance should be designated in advance of each new year. If a church fails to designate a parsonage allowance before the start of a new year, it is not lost for the entire new year. Rather, the church can designate a parsonage allowance at anytime during the year, for the remainder of that year. To illustrate, if a church discovers on March 10 that it has not yet designated a parsonage allowance for its pastor, it can do so on that date for the remainder of the year.

Many ministers who live in a parsonage are unaware that they do not pay tax on that portion of their salary that is designated in advance by their church as a parsonage allowance (to the extent that it is used to pay parsonage-related expenses). Such an allowance costs the church nothing, but it provides a minister with a significant tax benefit.

4. Social Security. The parsonage exclusion and parsonage allowance exclusion are exclusions for federal income tax purposes only. They cannot under any circumstances be excluded in computing a minister's Social Security (self-employment) taxes. Therefore, in computing self- employment taxes on Schedule SE (Form 1040) a minister who lives in a church-owned parsonage must include the annual rental value of the parsonage, as well as a parsonage allowance, as income.

What is the annual rental value of a parsonage. The IRS has simply said that "determining the fair rental value [of a parsonage] is a question of all facts and circumstances based on the local market."

5. Equity allowances. Ministers who live in church-owned parsonages experience a significant disadvantage—they do not acquire equity in a home. Some churches have helped ministers who live in parsonages avoid or at least reduce the adverse economic impact of this housing arrangement by providing them with an "equity allowance" over and above their stated compensation. This allowance is designed to partially or wholly compensate the minister for the "lost opportunity" of accumulating equity in a home. Since the purpose of such an allowance is to assist the minister in obtaining suitable housing at retirement, it is important that the allowance not be available to the minister until retirement. One way that churches can accomplish this is to deposit the annual equity allowance in a tax-favored retirement program not currently accessible to the minister. This is an excellent approach that can help to avoid a most unfortunate financial predicament for a minister who, often sacrificially, has devoted a lifetime to the church.

However, since an equity allowance does not compensate a minister for actual costs incurred in living in a parsonage, it is not excludable from income as a parsonage allowance.

QUIZ ANSWER KEY
1- True, 2-False, 3-True, 4-False, 5-True, 6-False

CHAPTER 7

How Do You Pay Estimated Taxes?

Estimated tax reporting procedures are confusing, but it's important that ministers understand them to avoid significant tax liabilities. In this chapter, we'll teach you how to determine if you should make estimated tax payments, and if so, how to comply with the estimated tax procedure.

Test your knowledge

Before we start, take a few minutes to complete the following quiz and find out how much you already know. You'll find the answer key at the end of the chapter. Don't worry if you don't know all the answers yet; you'll learn as you read the chapter.

QUIZ
Select true or false:

1. Pastor T's income tax return for last year (which was for the entire calendar year) showed a tax of $7,000. Pastor T projects that the tax to be shown on her current year's return will be $7,500. She also anticipates that no taxes will be withheld from her income as a minister this year (her only source of income). Pastor T is exempt from Social Security taxes. Pastor T is not required to pay estimated taxes.
   ❏ True   ❏ False

12 Law and Tax Guidelines for New Ministers

2. Pastor Y's income tax return for last year (which was for the entire calendar year) showed a tax of $7,000. Pastor Y has entered into a voluntary withholding agreement with his church, and estimates that $6,500 will be withheld from his compensation this year. Pastor Y is exempt from Social Security taxes. Pastor Y is not required to pay estimated taxes.
   ❏ True   ❏ False

3. Pastor H is senior minister at his church. The church board fails to designate a housing allowance until May of this year. Pastor H's April 15th estimated tax payment was based on his annual earnings less an anticipated housing allowance exclusion. The delayed designation of a housing allowance will almost certainly affect Pastor H's estimated taxes, and so he can re-compute the remaining three quarterly payments so that an underpayment penalty is avoided.
   ❏ True   ❏ False

4. Pastor J does not elect voluntary withholding of any taxes, and does not use the estimated tax procedure. Instead, he simply computes his taxes for the year and sends in a check with his Form 1040. As long as Pastor J sends in a check for the full amount of his taxes, he will not be assessed an underpayment penalty as a result of his failure to comply with the estimated tax procedure.
   ❏ True   ❏ False

How Do You Pay Estimated Taxes?

The Main Idea

Ministers' compensation is exempt from federal income tax withholding, whether they report their income taxes as employees or as self-employed. Ministers must prepay their income taxes and self-employment taxes using the estimated tax procedure (unless they elect voluntary withholding, which is addressed in Chapter 8 of this book).

Tax reporting procedure

New ministers should be familiar with the estimated tax reporting procedure for the following reasons:

- The wages of ministers who report their income taxes as employees are exempt from federal income tax withholding, and so these ministers must prepay their taxes using the estimated tax procedure (unless they request voluntary withholding).

- Ministers are self-employed for Social Security with respect to services they perform in the exercise of their ministry, and so they pay "self-employment taxes" (Social Security taxes paid by self-employed persons) rather than Social Security and Medicare taxes. Self-employment taxes are not withheld from a minister's wages, and so ministers pay these taxes using the estimated tax procedure unless they (1) report their income taxes as an employee, (2) request voluntary withholding of income taxes, and (3) request that an additional amount of income taxes be withheld that will be sufficient to cover the anticipated self-employment tax liability for the year.

- Churches never withhold income taxes from the wages of ministers who are self-employed for federal income tax reporting purposes, and so these ministers must prepay their taxes using the estimated tax procedure.

The exemption of ministers from income tax withholding, coupled with an unfamiliarity with the estimated tax requirements, has caused many younger and inexperienced ministers to refrain from reporting or paying their taxes. It is essential that ministers be familiar with the rules discussed below.

NOTE
Estimated taxes are computed and reported on IRS Form 1040-ES.

Who should make estimated tax payments?
Generally, you should make estimated tax payments if your estimated tax for this year will be $1,000 or more and the total amount of income tax that will be withheld from your income will be less than the lesser of (1) 90% of your tax liability for the current year, or (2) 100% of your tax liability for the previous year (if it covered all twelve months of the year).

If you are required to pay estimated taxes, but fail to do so, you will be subject to an "underpayment penalty." Since the penalty is figured separately for each quarterly period, you may owe a penalty for an earlier payment period even if you later paid enough to make up the underpayment. If you did not pay enough tax by the due date of each of the payment periods, you may owe a penalty even if you are due a refund when you file your income tax return!

The 4-step procedure for paying estimated taxes

Complying with the estimated tax procedure is easy. Here are the four steps you need to follow:

Step 1– Obtain a copy of IRS Form 1040-ES. Obtain a copy of IRS Form 1040-ES prior to April 15 of the current year. You will note that Form 1040-ES consists of a worksheet, instructions, and four dated "payment vouchers." You can obtain a copy from any IRS office, the IRS website, many public libraries, or by calling the toll-free IRS forms "hotline" at 1-800-TAX-FORM (1-800-829-3676).

Step 2–Compute estimated taxes. Compute your estimated tax for the current year using the Form 1040-ES worksheet. This is done by estimating adjusted gross income and then subtracting estimated adjustments, deductions, exemptions, and credits. Using your previous year's tax return is a helpful starting point. To determine your estimated taxes, multiply estimated taxable income times the applicable tax rate contained in the Tax Rate Schedule reproduced on Form 1040-ES. Remember to include your estimated Social Security tax on the worksheet if you are not exempt, and to include your housing allowance exclusion in computing your estimated earnings subject to the self-employment tax (the housing allowance is excluded from income only in computing your income tax liability, not your self-employment tax).

Step 3–Pay estimated taxes in quarterly installments. If estimated taxes (federal income taxes and self-employment taxes) are more than $1,000 for the current year, and the total amount of taxes to be withheld from your compensation is less than the lesser of (1)

90% of your tax liability for the current year, or (2) 100% of your tax liability for the previous year, then you must pay one-fourth of your total estimated taxes in four quarterly installments as follows:

For the Period	Due Date
Jan. 1- Mar. 31	April 15
April 1- May 31	June 15
June 1- Aug. 31	September 15
Sep. 1- Dec. 31	January 15

If the due date for making an estimated tax payment falls on a Saturday, Sunday, or legal holiday, the payment will be on time if you make it on the next day that is not a Saturday, Sunday, or legal holiday.

> *Payment vouchers.* You must send each payment to the IRS, accompanied by one of the four payment vouchers contained in Form 1040-ES. If you paid estimated taxes last year, you should receive a copy of your current year's Form 1040-ES in the mail with payment vouchers preprinted with your name, address, and Social Security number. If you did not pay estimated taxes last year, you will have to get a copy of Form 1040-ES from the IRS. After you make your first payment (April 15) you should receive a Form 1040-ES package in your name with the preprinted information. There is a separate payment voucher for each of the four quarterly payment periods. Each one has the due date printed on it. Be sure to use the correct payment voucher.

Starting a job in mid-year. A minister may become liable for estimated tax payments midway through a year. For example, a minister may change churches midway through a year, leaving a church that voluntarily withheld taxes and going to another church that does not withhold taxes. In such a case, the minister should submit a payment voucher by the next filing deadline accompanied by a check for a prorated portion of the entire estimated tax liability for the year.

Changing your quarterly payments. After making your first or second estimated tax payment, changes in your income, deductions, credits, or exemptions may make it necessary for you to refigure your estimated tax and adjust your remaining quarterly payments accordingly.

Step 4–Compute actual taxes. After the close of the year you will compute your actual tax liability on Form 1040. Only then will you know your actual income, deductions, exclusions, and credits. Estimated tax payments rarely reflect actual tax liability. Most taxpayers' estimated tax payments are either more or less than actual taxes as computed on Form 1040 (usually less). The consequences of overpayment and underpayment of estimated taxes is summarized below.

Overpayment. If you overpaid your estimated taxes (i.e., your estimated tax payments plus any withholding were more than your actual taxes computed on Form 1040) you can elect to have the overpayment credited against your first quarterly estimated tax payment of the following year or spread out in any way you choose among any or all of your next four quarterly installments. Alternatively, you can request a refund of the overpayment.

Underpayment. If you underpaid your estimated taxes (i.e., your estimated tax payments plus any withholding were less than your actual taxes computed on Form 1040) you may have to pay a penalty. In general, you may owe a penalty if you do not pay at least the smaller of (1) 90% of your tax liability for the current year, or (2) 100% of your tax liability for the previous year (if it covered the entire year). The penalty is computed separately for each quarterly payment period. Contrary to popular belief, payment of your entire estimated tax liability with your Form 1040 will not relieve you of the penalty if you did not pay the estimated income tax due earlier in the year.

Form 2210. You can use Form 2210 to see if you owe a penalty and to figure the amount of the penalty. If you owe a penalty and do not attach Form 2210 to your Form 1040, the IRS will compute your penalty and send you a bill. You do not have to fill out a Form 2210 or pay any penalty if either of two conditions apply: (1) your total tax less income tax withheld is less than $1,000, or (2) you had no tax liability last year and you were a United States citizen or resident for the entire year. The IRS can waive the underpayment penalty if the underpayment was due to casualty, disaster, or other unusual circumstance and it would be inequitable to impose the penalty.

Special rule for high-income taxpayers. High-income taxpayers cannot avoid the underpayment penalty by paying estimated taxes for the current year of at least 100 percent of last year's tax. A high-income taxpayer is one with adjusted gross income for the previous year of at least $150,000. For such persons, the "100 percent rule" is replaced with a 110 percent rule, meaning that they will be subject to an underpayment penalty unless they have paid estimated taxes for the current year of at least the lesser of (1) 90 percent of the current year's actual tax liability, or (2) 110 percent of last year's actual tax liability.

QUIZ ANSWER KEY
False, 2-False, 3-True, 4-False

CHAPTER 8

Can You Have the Church Withhold Your Taxes?

Even if you report your income taxes as self-employed, there are ways for you to have your taxes withheld. This chapter will explain why you might want to request voluntary withholding, and how to go about having taxes withheld.

Test your knowledge

Before we start, take a few minutes to complete the following quiz and find out how much you already know. You'll find the answer key at the end of the chapter. Don't worry if you don't know all the answers yet; you'll learn as you read the chapter.

QUIZ
Select true or false:

1. Pastor B is an ordained minister who is currently employed as a church custodian. Since Pastor B is a minister, the church treasurer does not withhold federal income taxes from his wages. The church treasurer is correct in concluding that Pastor B's wages are not subject to income tax withholding.
❏ True   ❏ False

2. Wages paid to a minister for services performed in the exercise of ministry are not subject to federal income tax withholding.
❏ True ❏ False

3. Pastor C is senior pastor of his church. He reports his federal income taxes as an employee. He requests voluntary withholding of his income taxes. The church treasurer assumes that if he withholds income taxes from Pastor C's wages, he is required to withhold Social Security and Medicare taxes. Is the church treasurer correct?
❏ True ❏ False

4. Pastors who report their federal income taxes as employees and who request voluntary withholding may have an additional amount of income taxes withheld to cover their self-employment tax liability for the year.
❏ True ❏ False

The Main Idea

Ministers are exempt from federal tax withholding, whether they report their income taxes as an employee or as self-employed. However, if they report their income taxes as an employee, they may request "voluntary withholding" of their income taxes and self-employment taxes by filing a Form W-4 with the church. A self-employed minister is free to enter into an "unofficial" withholding arrangement whereby the church withholds a portion of

> his or her compensation each week and deposits it in a church account, and then distributes the balance to the minister in advance of each quarterly estimated tax payment due date.

What you need to know

The federal income tax is a "pay as you go" tax. This means that you must pay your tax as you earn income during the year. There are two ways to do this—tax withholding and quarterly estimated tax payments. This lesson addresses tax withholding and its application to new ministers.

Most employers are required to withhold federal income taxes from employees' wages as they are paid. But there are exceptions, including wages paid for "services performed by a duly ordained, commissioned, or licensed minister of a church in the exercise of his ministry." As a result, a church is not required to withhold income taxes from wages paid to ministers who report and pay their income taxes as employees. This exemption only applies to "services performed in the exercise of ministry."

Ministers who are self-employed for income tax purposes report and prepay their income taxes and Social Security taxes by means of the estimated tax procedure (discussed in Chapter 7). Self-employed persons are not subject to tax withholding.

The IRS audit guidelines for ministers contain the following statement regarding the application of tax withholding to ministers: "Although they are generally considered employees under the common law rules, payment for services as a minister is considered income from self employment and is not subject to FICA taxes or income tax withholding (if the employer and employee agree, an election can be made to have income taxes withheld)." The IRS audit guidelines are used by IRS agents when auditing ministers.

Voluntary withholding

Ministers who report their income taxes as an employee can enter into a "voluntary" withholding arrangement with their church. Under such an arrangement, the church withholds federal income taxes from the minister's wages just as it would for any nonminister employee. Some ministers find voluntary withholding attractive since it avoids the additional work and discipline associated with the estimated tax procedure.

How is a voluntary withholding arrangement initiated? A minister who elects to enter into a voluntary withholding arrangement with his or her church need only file a completed IRS Form W-4 (employee's withholding allowance certificate) with the church. The filing of this form is deemed to be a request for voluntary withholding.

Voluntary withholding arrangements may be terminated at any time by either the church or minister, or by mutual consent of both. Alternatively, a minister can stipulate that the voluntary withholding arrangement terminates on a specified date. Of course, a voluntary withholding arrangement will affect the church's quarterly Form 941 since the church will include the minister's withheld income taxes on line 3.

What about a minister's self-employment taxes? Remember that ministers are always deemed to be self-employed for Social Security purposes with respect to services performed in the exercise of ministry. As a result, a church whose minister elects voluntary withholding is only obligated to withhold the minister's federal income tax liability. The minister is still required to use the estimated tax procedure to report and prepay the self-employment tax (the Social Security tax on self-employed persons). Such a result is unsatisfactory since it still requires the minister to file quarterly estimated tax payments (Form 1040-ES).

Consider the following alternative. Ministers who report their income taxes as employees (and who are not exempt from Social Security) should consider filing an amended W-4 form (withholding allowance certificate) with their church, indicating on line 6 an additional amount of cash to be withheld from each pay period that will be sufficient to pay the estimated self-employment tax liability by the end of the year. IRS Publication 517 states that "if you perform your services as an employee of the church (under the common law rules), you may be able to enter into a voluntary withholding agreement with your employer, the church, to cover any income and self-employment tax that may be due."

A church whose minister has elected voluntary withholding (and who is not exempt from Social Security taxes) simply withholds an additional amount from each paycheck to cover the minister's estimated self-employment tax liability for the year, and then reports this additional amount as additional income tax (not "Social Security" or "Medicare" tax) withheld on its quarterly 941 forms that are filed with the IRS as well as on the minister's W-2 form at the end of the year. The excess income tax withheld is a credit against tax that the minister claims on his or her federal income tax return (Form 1040), and is applied to the minister's self-employment tax liability. Since any tax paid by voluntary withholding is deemed to be timely paid, a minister who pays self-employment taxes using this procedure will not be liable for any underpayment penalty assuming that a sufficient amount of taxes are in fact withheld. Ministers who report their income taxes as employees should consider the convenience of voluntary withholding with respect to both income taxes and self-employment taxes.

A self-employed minister is free to enter into an "unofficial" withholding arrangement whereby the church withholds a portion of his or her compensation each week and deposits it in a church account, and then distributes the balance to the minister in advance of each quarterly estimated tax payment due date. No W-4 forms should be used, and the "withholdings" are not reported on Form 941.

QUIZ ANSWER KEY
1- False, 2-True, 3-False, 4-True

CHAPTER 9

What Is the Best Way for You to Handle Business Expenses?

You'll likely incur business expenses as you conduct your ministry. In this chapter, you'll learn about accountable reimbursement arrangements and how to properly report expenses.

Test your knowledge

Before we start, take a few minutes to complete the following quiz and find out how much you already know. You'll find the answer key at the end of the chapter. Don't worry if you don't know all the answers yet; you'll learn as you read the chapter.

QUIZ
Select true or false:

1. Pastor M pays for business expenses that he incurs throughout the year. During the last week of the year he presents the church treasurer with a shoebox full of receipts that document the expenses he incurred. The church treasurer issues him a check for this amount. This an accountable reimbursement arrangement since the pastor is properly accounting for all of his business expenses, and so the reimbursement check would not

be reported as taxable income to Pastor M.
❏ True   ❏ False

2. A pastor provides the church treasurer with a statement each month showing the total amount of business expenses he paid for during the previous month. The church's reimbursements of these monthly statements is nonaccountable.
❏ True   ❏ False

3. A church provides its pastor with a credit card. The pastor charges expenses to the card each month, but is not required to account for the business nature of every expense. This is an example of a nonaccountable reimbursement arrangement, meaning that all of the church's reimbursements would have to be reported as taxable income to the pastor.
❏ True   ❏ False

4. A church provides its pastor with a cash advance of $2,000 for a trip to a church conference in another state. The pastor incurs only $1,200 of expenses while on this trip, but is not required to return the excess reimbursement of $800 to the church. The $800 represents a nonaccountable reimbursement that must be reported as taxable income to the pastor.
❏ True   ❏ False

5. A church establishes its pastor's compensation for the new year as follows: salary of $30,000, housing allowance of $10,000, and business expense reimbursement account of $5,000, for "total compensation" of $45,000. The church reimburses $5,000

of the pastor's business expenses during the year. This is an accountable arrangement, so the expense reimbursements would not be reported as taxable income to the pastor.

❏ True   ❏ False

The Main Idea

Most individuals engaged in ministry pay for business expenses in the course of their employment. Common examples would be local business travel, out-of-town trips, entertainment, supplies, and publications. Our research shows that most churches reimburse at least some of the business expenses their staff members incur. As a new minister, you should understand that there are two ways for a church to reimburse your business expenses—through either an accountable or a nonaccountable arrangement. Under an accountable arrangement, a church reimburses only those business expenses that are properly "accounted for." The requirements for such an arrangement are addressed in this lesson. If your church has implemented an accountable arrangement, then none of the reimbursements it pays to you are reported as taxable income. Further, you have no expenses to deduct. You in effect are reporting your business expenses to your employer rather than to the IRS. Such a system requires vigilance. If your church treats your reimbursements as accountable, but you fail to meet the requirements summarized in this lesson, then you have received unreported taxable income.

What you need to know

An accountable business expense reimbursement arrangement is the most desirable way for a church to handle a minister's business expenses. Church reimbursements are not reported as taxable income to the minister, and there are no unreimbursed expenses of the minister to deduct. The employee, in effect, accounts to the church rather than to the IRS. To be accountable, a church's reimbursement arrangement must include all four of the following rules:

1. Business connection. A reimbursement arrangement meets the business connection requirement if it only reimburses employee expenses that could be claimed by the employee as a business expense deduction, and that are paid or incurred by the employee in connection with the performance of services as an employee.

2. Adequate accounting. You must adequately account to your employer for any business expense that it reimburses. In general, this means that you must submit an expense account or other written statement to the employer showing the date, amount, location, and business connection of all your expenses (including those charged directly or indirectly to the employer through credit cards) broken down into categories such as transportation, meals and lodging while away from home overnight, entertainment expenses, and other business expenses. Receipts are required for any expense of more than $75.

An employee's "accounting" or substantiation of business expenses must occur within a reasonable time. In general, this means that expenses are substantiated within 60 days of when they are incurred.

What Is the Best Way for You to Handle Business Expenses?

Some churches agree to reimburse all of their minister's substantiated business expenses without limitation. Others reimburse substantiated expenses up to a fixed limit (e.g., $4,000 per year). Any business expenses incurred by the minister in excess of this amount would be unreimbursed.

A question that often arises is who owns property purchased by a minister or lay employee if the purchase price is reimbursed by the church under an accountable arrangement. In general, when an employer reimburses an employee for the cost of property purchased by the employee for business use, it is the employer rather than the employee that is the legal owner of the property. After all, property purchased by an employee cannot be reimbursed under an accountable arrangement unless the employee substantiates the cost and business purpose of the property. In other words, it must be clear that the property will be used solely for the business purposes of the employer. Under these circumstances, there is little doubt as a matter of law that the employer is the legal owner of the property. The employer paid for it, and the accountable nature of the reimbursement arrangement ensures that it will be used by the employee within the course of his or her employment on behalf of the employer. In many cases, the value of property diminishes rapidly, and in a sense is "used up" within a period of months or a few years. As a result, the question of "ownership" of the property when the employee leaves his or her job has little relevance, since the value is so minimal.

You can keep an adequate record for parts of a tax year and use that record to prove the amount of business or investment use for the entire year. You must demonstrate by other evidence that the periods for which an adequate record is kept are representative of the use throughout the tax year. For example, assume that you keep adequate records during the first week of each month that show that 75% of the use of your car is for business. Invoices and bills show that your business use continues at the same rate during the later weeks of each month.

Your weekly records are representative of the use of the car each month and are sufficient evidence to support the percentage of business use for the year.

3. Returning excess reimbursements. You must return any excess reimbursement or allowance within a reasonable period of time (not more than 120 days after an excess reimbursement is paid). An excess reimbursement or allowance is any amount you are paid that is more than the business-related expenses that you adequately accounted for to your employer.

4. Reimbursements not made out of salary reductions. The income tax regulations caution that in order for an employer's reimbursement arrangement to be accountable, it must meet a reimbursement requirement in addition to the three requirements summarized above. The reimbursement requirement means that an employer's reimbursements of an employee's business expenses come out of the employer's funds and not by reducing or "restructuring" the employee's salary.

The IRS has issued audit guidelines for its agents to follow when auditing ministers. The guidelines inform agents that if a church has a salary reduction arrangement which "reimburses" a minister for employee business expenses by reducing his or her salary, the arrangement will be treated as a nonaccountable plan. This is the result:

Regardless of whether a specific portion of the minister's compensation is designated for employee expenses or whether the portion of the compensation to be treated as the expense allowance varies from pay period to pay period depending on the minister's expenses. As long as the minister is entitled to receive the full amount of annual compensation, regardless of whether or not any employee business expenses are incurred during the taxable year, the arrangement does not meet the reimbursement requirement.

The guidelines instruct IRS agents to be alert to salary reduction arrangements that are used to fund reimbursements under an "accountable" arrangement. According to the IRS, accountable plans cannot reimburse employee business expenses out of salary reductions. The important point is this—the guidelines are educating IRS agents as to this issue, and so it is now far more likely that salary restructuring and salary reduction arrangements will be discovered and questioned in an audit.

QUIZ ANSWER KEY
1- False, 2-True, 3-True, 4-True, 5-False

CHAPTER 10

What Is the Clergy-Penitent Privilege?

The clergy-penitent privilege is often a source of confusion for ministers. Whether a communication is privileged depends on several factors. This chapter will explain what the clergy-penitent privilege is and how to determine if a communication is privileged.

Test your knowledge

Before we start, take a few minutes to complete the following quiz and find out how much you already know. You'll find the answer key at the end of the chapter. Don't worry if you don't know all the answers yet; you'll learn as you read the chapter.

QUIZ
Choose the best answer:

1. While playing golf with his pastor, a church member confesses to an unsolved crime. Is this confession privileged?
   (a) No. Conversations that occur in the midst of a social activity cannot be privileged.
   (b) No. The pastor was not acting as a spiritual adviser.
   (c) Yes. Confessions made to pastors always are privileged.
   (d) Yes, if the member was communicating to the pastor as a spiritual adviser at the time of the confession.

2. A church member discusses a personal problem with a church board member in the church library following a worship service. Is this conversation privileged?

   (a) No. Conversations with church board members who are not ministers cannot be privileged.

   (b) No. The conversation was not confidential.

   (c) Yes, if no third parties were present.

   (d) Yes, if the member was communicating to the board member as a spiritual adviser at the time of the confession.

3. Which of the following statements are true?

   (a) The clergy-penitent privilege can apply to telephone conversations between a pastor and church member.

   (b) The clergy-penitent privilege can apply to letters between a pastor and church member.

   (c) Both A and B.

   (d) Neither A nor B.

4. Which of the following statements is true?

   (a) The clergy-penitent privilege does not apply to conversations that a pastor has with persons who are not members of the pastor's church.

   (b) In many states pastors are not required to report to civil authorities incidents of child abuse they learn of in the course of a conversation protected by the clergy-penitent privilege.

   (c) Pastors can ignore a subpoena requesting their testimony in court if they will be asked to disclose the contents of a conversation that is protected by the clergy-penitent privilege.

   (d) The clergy-penitent privilege applies to a pastor's impressions of the "demeanor" of a counselee.

The Main Idea

Certain communications that are made to ministers, in confidence, are "privileged." This means that the minister, or counselee, cannot be forced to disclose the content of the communications in a court of law. Ministers often are asked to testify in court in criminal trials regarding conversations they had with a criminal defendant, or in divorce cases regarding conversations they had with one of the spouses, and so new ministers should be familiar with the basic requirements of the "clergy-penitent" privilege.

What you need to know

Every new minister should be familiar with the clergy-penitent privilege. This chapter provides an overview of the most important considerations.

Privilege

Just what is a "privilege"? A privilege refers to evidence that is not admissible in court. There are many examples, including communications made in confidence between an attorney and client, a doctor and patient, a husband and wife, and a minister and penitent. The basis for the clergy-penitent privilege is that we want people to communicate freely with their minister without fear of having their conversation disclosed in court. After all, without this assurance few would be willing to share potentially incriminating information with their minister, and this is not a socially desirable result.

Requirements

Not every communication made to a minister is privileged. In most states, the clergy- penitent privilege applies only to (1) communications (2) confidentially made (3) to a minister (4) acting in a professional capacity as a spiritual adviser. Let's look at each of these requirements more closely.

1. **Communication.** The privilege applies only to "communications" between an individual and a minister. Communications obviously include verbal statements, but they also can include nonverbal acts that are intended to transmit ideas. To illustrate, one court ruled that a counselee who pulled a gun out of his pocket and placed it on the pastor's desk in response to the pastor's question about a recent murder had made a "communication." Other courts have ruled that a pastor's impressions of a counselee's demeanor are not communications because one's demeanor is not a communication. Statements made over the telephone, or in a letter, generally will be "communications."

2. **Confidential.** A communication must be made in confidence to be privileged. This means that it was made under circumstances indicating that it would remain secret. Statements made to a minister in the presence of other persons generally cannot be privileged. However, if the presence of a third person is legally required (e.g., a prisoner who cannot communicate with a minister unless a guard is present), the privilege may apply. Several state laws extend the clergy-penitent privilege to situations in which other persons are present "in furtherance of the communication." This probably would include

marital counseling sessions when both spouses are present. Also, some ministers do not engage in opposite sex counseling without a third person being present. Will the presence of such a third person mean that statements made to the minister are not privileged (because they are no longer confidential)? Such a conclusion is certainly possible. But in states that preserve the privilege when third persons are present "in furtherance of the communication" the argument certainly can be made that the presence of the third person in such a situation is "in furtherance of the purpose of the communication," particularly if the church board adopted a resolution prohibiting opposite sex counseling by ministers without a third person being present. However, statements made to a minister in the presence of deacons, elders, church members, or any other persons will not be privileged, unless specifically recognized by state law.

3. To a minister. In order to be privileged, a communication must be made to a minister. Communications made to church board members, a minister's spouse, or "lay ministers" cannot be privileged.

4. Acting in a professional capacity as a spiritual adviser. Most clergy-penitent privilege laws require that the communication be made to a minister acting in a professional capacity as a spiritual adviser. Certainly there can be no expectation of confidentiality—and therefore no privilege—unless a statement is made to a minister acting in such a capacity. If a statement is made to a minister as a mere friend, the privilege does not apply. Many, perhaps most, of the communications made to ministers are not made to them in their professional capacity as spiritual advisers. They are made by church members and nonmembers alike at church functions, following church services, in committee rooms, in hospital rooms, at funeral homes, in restaurants, on street corners, and at social and recreational events. Such communications ordinarily are not privileged, since other persons typically are present, and it is difficult to conclude that the "counselee" sought out the minister in his or her professional capacity as a spiritual adviser. Of course, it is entirely possible that such conversations, even if they began as a purely social exchange, could become spiritual in nature. In other words, by the end of a conversation the "counselee" may well be communicating with the minister because of his or her status as a spiritual adviser. There is no reason why such a conversation should not be privileged, assuming that the other requirements are satisfied. On the other hand, even strictly private conversations may be made for purposes other than spiritual advice.

A minister (or court) may need to ascertain the objective of a conversation in determining whether a communication is privileged. Was the minister sought out primarily for spiritual advice? Were the statements of a type that could have been made to anyone? Where did the conversation take place? Was the conversation pursuant to a scheduled appointment? What was the relationship between the minister and the person making the communication? These are the kinds of questions which help to clarify the purpose of a particular conversation, thereby determining the availability of the privilege. The applicability of the privilege can be enhanced if a minister simply asks a person during a counseling session whether he or she intends for the conversation to be privileged and confidential. If the counselee responds affirmatively, then there is little doubt that the courts will conclude that the privilege applies. Ministers should bear this point in mind in the course of their counseling. If, during a conversation with a member (wherever it may occur), it appears to a minister that the other person may intend for the conversation to be confidential and privileged, the minister should confirm this understanding verbally. If the minister is ever called to testify in court concerning the conversation, this verbal confirmation should resolve most questions regarding the applicability of the clergy-penitent privilege.

Who asserts the privilege

In most states, both the person who made the communication and the minister to whom it was made may claim the privilege. Rule 505 of the Uniform Rules of Evidence, which has been adopted by several states, specifies that "the privilege may be claimed by the person, by his guardian or conservator, or by his personal representative if he is deceased. The person who was the clergyman at the time of the communication is presumed to have authority to claim the privilege but only on behalf of the communicant." However, in some states, only the penitent or "counselee" may assert the privilege, not the minister.

When to assert the privilege

The clergy-penitent privilege does not excuse ministers from appearing in court. Rather, it excuses them from disclosing a privileged communication in court against their will. The proper time to assert the privilege is in court (or at a deposition) when asked to disclose communications protected by the privilege. Of course, ministers do not technically "object" to such a question. The attorney for one of the parties to the underlying legal action ordinarily will object to the question in order to prevent the minister from disclosing the privileged communication. In some cases no objection is made. In such a case ministers are free to inform the judge that they prefer not to answer the question on the ground that it seeks privileged information.

For further help

As this lesson illustrates, it is imperative for new ministers to be familiar with their own state's clergy-penitent privilege. The text of every state's clergy-penitent privilege statute is reproduced in Appendix 3 of Richard Hammar's book, *Pastor, Church & Law, Volume 1: Legal Issues for Pastors* (4th ed. 2008), and is also updated periodically in the bimonthly newsletter *Church Law & Tax Report*.

QUIZ ANSWER KEY
1-D, 2-A, 3-C, 4-B

CHAPTER 11

Are You Required to Report Child Abuse?

Unfortunately, ministers often learn of the abuse of minors. As a new minister, you should be aware of the laws that govern child abuse reporting, and the consequences of reporting or not reporting suspected abuse. In this chapter, we'll help you understand child abuse reporting laws.

Test your knowledge

Before we start, take a few minutes to complete the following quiz and find out how much you already know. You'll find the answer key at the end of the chapter. Don't worry if you don't know all the answers yet; you'll learn as you read the chapter.

QUIZ
Select true or false:

1. A *mandatory* child abuse reporter is legally required to report known or reasonably suspected cases of child abuse.
   ❏ True   ❏ False

2. Pastors are mandatory child abuse reporters in all states.
   ❏ True   ❏ False

3. Permissive reporters are persons who are not mandatory reporters. They are permitted to report, but are not legally required to do so.
   ❏ True   ❏ False

4. Tim is the senior pastor at his church. He also teaches a few courses at a private school operated by the church. Pastor Tim learns of an incident of child abuse from one of his students. As a pastor, he is not legally required to report this incident to civil authorities.
   ❏ True   ❏ False

5. Mandatory reporters who know of an incident of child abuse, or who have reasonable cause to believe that such an incident has occurred, are subject to criminal penalties if they do not comply with their state's child abuse reporting law.
   ❏ True   ❏ False

6. Pastor Ron is the senior pastor of his church. He learns of an allegation of child abuse involving a member of the church's youth group. Pastor Ron can be personally liable if he reports the allegation to civil authorities and it is proven to be unfounded.
   ❏ True   ❏ False

7. Pastor Todd is the senior pastor of his church. A 13-year-old girl meets with Pastor Todd and informs him that she is being sexually molested by her stepfather. If Pastor Todd is a mandatory child abuse reporter, he must report this information to the civ-

il authorities.
❏ True   ❏ False

8. Child abuse reporting laws only apply to incidents of child abuse involving children under 13 years of age.
❏ True   ❏ False

The Main Idea

It is essential for new ministers to be familiar with child abuse reporting requirements under state law. Unfamiliarity with these requirements can lead to criminal and civil liability.

Ministers sometimes learn that a minor is being abused. This can occur in a number of ways, including a disclosure by the victim or a friend or relative of the victim, or a confession by the perpetrator. Often, ministers assume that they can resolve such matters by counseling with the victim or the alleged offender, without contacting civil authorities. Such a response can have serious legal consequences. Ministers who are mandatory reporters under state law face possible criminal prosecution for failing to comply with their state's child abuse reporting law. Ministers can also sometimes be sued by child abuse victims for failing to report child abuse.

As a result, it is imperative for ministers to be able to answer the following questions:

1. What is the definition of reportable "child abuse" under my state child abuse reporting law?
2. Am I a mandatory reporter of child abuse?
3. What if I learn of child abuse in the course of a conversation that is protected by the clergy-penitent privilege? Am I still required to report?
4. How do I report child abuse?

Each of these questions is addressed below.

What is child abuse?

All 50 states have enacted child abuse reporting statutes in an effort to protect abused children and prevent future abuse. Child abuse is defined by most statutes to include physical abuse, emotional abuse, neglect, and sexual molestation. A child ordinarily is defined as any person under the age of 18 years. Some states specifically limit the definition of "child abuse" to abuse that is inflicted by a parent, caretaker, or custodian. Such a statute, if interpreted narrowly, might not require ministers and lay church workers who are mandatory reporters of child abuse under state law to report incidents of abuse inflicted by custodians, associate ministers, adolescents, or volunteer youth workers.

Who are mandatory reporters of child abuse?

All 50 states identify those persons who are under a legal duty to report abuse to designated civil authorities. In most states, such "mandatory reporters" must report both actual and reasonably suspected cases of child abuse. Failure to do so is a crime (usually a misdemeanor). Some states define mandatory reporters to include any person having a reasonable belief that child abuse has occurred. Obviously, ministers will be mandatory reporters under these statutes. The remaining states define mandatory reporters by referring to a list of occupations which generally includes physicians, dentists, hospital employees, nurses, coroners, school employees, nursery school workers, law enforcement officers, and licensed psychologists. Ministers are specifically identified as mandatory reporters in most states. But even if they are not, they may be mandatory reporters if they fall within a listed classification, such as school or child care workers and administrators, or counselors. In summary, ministers are mandatory reporters of child abuse under the laws of most states, and should never assume that they have no duty to report.

Pastors who are not mandatory reporters under their state's law generally are considered "permissive reporters," meaning that they are encouraged to report cases of abuse to the designated civil authorities but are not legally required to do so.

Pastors often ask if they can be liable if they report a suspected incident of child abuse that later proves to be unfounded. The answer to this question is that every state grants "limited immunity" to reporters of child abuse. This means that reporters cannot be sued simply for reporting child abuse, unless they do so "maliciously." The reason that every state provides legal immunity to reporters is to encourage child abuse reporting.

The fact that you are not a mandatory reporter of child abuse under state law does not mean that you should not report known or reasonably suspected incidents of abuse or molestation. Many ministers who are not mandatory reporters choose to report abuse, especially if the evidence is strong and the victim is young, or to protect other minors from being molested.

What if I learn of child abuse in the course of a conversation that is protected by the clergy-penitent privilege?

Pastors who are mandatory reporters of child abuse under state law are under a profound ethical dilemma when they receive information about child abuse in the course of a confidential counseling session that is subject to the clergy-penitent privilege. They have to choose to either fulfill their legal obligation to report or to honor their ecclesiastical duty to maintain the confidentiality of privileged communications. A number of states have attempted to resolve this dilemma by specifically exempting ministers from the duty to report child abuse if the abuse is disclosed to them in the course of a communication protected by the clergy-penitent privilege. Other states, while not specifically excluding ministers from the duty to report, specify that information protected by the clergy-penitent privilege is not admissible in any legal proceeding regarding the alleged abuse. Some state child abuse reporting statutes do not list the clergy-penitent privilege among those privileges that are abolished in the context of child abuse proceedings. The intent of such statutes may be to excuse ministers from testifying in such cases regarding information they learned in the course of a privileged communication.

Even if the clergy-penitent privilege applies in the context of child abuse reporting, it is by no means clear that the privilege will be a defense to a failure to report, since (1) the information causing a minister to suspect that abuse has occurred may not have been privileged (that is, it was not obtained in confidence, or it was not obtained during spiritual counseling); and (2) a privilege ordinarily applies only to courtroom testimony or depositions, and not to a statutory requirement to report to a state agency.

How to report

Persons who are legally required to report child abuse generally make their report by notifying a designated state agency by telephone and confirming the telephone call with a written report within a prescribed period of time. The reporter generally is required to (1) identify the child, the child's parents or guardians, and the alleged abuser by name, and provide their addresses; (2) give the child's age; and (3) describe the nature of the abuse. Most states have toll-free numbers that receive initial reports of child abuse.

In short, ministers should be able to answer the questions raised in this lesson on the basis of the child abuse reporting law of their state. Unfortunately, child abuse reporting laws often are difficult to understand because they consist of several pages of legal jargon. To assist ministers in understanding their state's child abuse reporting law, see the biannually updated Feature Report titled "Child Abuse Reporting Laws," which summarizes the child abuse reporting laws of all 50 states. This article contains a table that answers each of the four questions mentioned earlier in this chapter. As a new minister, you should be familiar with the material in this article.

QUIZ ANSWER KEY
1- True, 2-False, 3-True, 4-False, 5-True, 6-False, 7-False, 8-False

CHAPTER 12

What Legal Requirements Apply to the Performance of Marriage Ceremonies?

Before performing a marriage ceremony, you should take steps to make sure you're authorized to perform the marriage and that the couple can legally marry. Laws pertaining to marriage ceremonies vary by state. In this chapter, we'll mention some of the factors you should consider in advance of a marriage ceremony and give you steps to take to make sure the marriage is legal.

Test your knowledge

Before we start, take a few minutes to complete the following quiz and find out how much you already know. You'll find the answer key at the end of the chapter. Don't worry if you don't know all the answers yet; you'll learn as you read the chapter.

QUIZ
Choose the best answer:

1. A pastor is asked by a family to conduct a marriage for their daughter in another state. Is the pastor legally authorized to perform this marriage?
    (a) Yes. Ministers can perform marriages in any state.
    (b) Yes, but only if the pastor is an ordained minister.

(c) Perhaps. It will depend on the law of the state in which the marriage will be performed. The pastor should check with civil authorities in the other state well before the marriage to be sure.

(d) No. Pastors are only legally authorized to perform marriages in their state of residence.

2. A youth pastor is licensed, but not ordained. Can the youth pastor perform a marriage for a former member of the youth group?

   (a) Yes. Ministers can perform marriages in any state, whether they are ordained or licensed.

   (b) Yes, but only if the pastor is employed full-time by the church.

   (c) Perhaps. It will depend on state law. The pastor should check with civil authorities well before the marriage to be sure that licensed pastors are legally authorized to perform marriages.

   (d) No. Licensed pastors never can perform marriages.

3. In most states, marriages must comply with certain legal requirements. It is important for pastors to be familiar with these requirements. They often include:

   (a) Premarital counseling.

   (b) The couple must have a valid and unexpired license issued by a government agency.

   (c) Both A and B.

   (d) Neither A nor B.

4. Pastors should have a premarital checklist to be sure they are

complying with legal requirements. This checklist should include which of the following items?

(a) Am I legally qualified to perform a marriage according to the law of my state?

(b) Is the engaged couple legally capable of marrying?

(c) Be sure that the couple has a valid marriage license with an expiration date later than the date of the marriage.

(d) All of the above.

> **The Main Idea**
>
> Ministers often are called upon to perform marriages for relatives, friends, and members of their congregation. The law regards marriage as a fundamental institution, and as a result imposes several conditions on the performance of the marriage ceremony. It is important for new ministers to be familiar with these conditions. Ministers are legally authorized to perform marriage ceremonies in every state. There are, however, a number of legal issues with which ministers should be familiar. These issues are summarized in this chapter.

Am I a "minister" who is authorized to solemnize marriages?

State laws vary widely in defining those ministers who are authorized to perform marriages. Some states require that the minister be ordained; others require that the minister be either licensed or ordained; and others omit any specific reference to either licensure or ordination. Be sure to check your state law to be sure you meet the definition of a minister for purposes of performing marriage ceremonies. Your county recorder's office often can help. Some states require ministers to register with a government agency before they are authorized to perform marriage ceremonies. Prior to performing marriage ceremonies, ministers should know whether or not such a requirement exists.

Can I perform a marriage in another state?

A family in your church wants you to perform the marriage ceremony for their child who is going to be married in another state. Are you authorized to do so? With the increasing mobility of American families, this is a question that frequently arises. The answer to this question will depend upon the law of the state in which the marriage will be performed. In many states, any minister is eligible to perform a marriage regardless of his or her state of residence. Other states have enacted laws authorizing nonresident ministers to perform a marriage within the state if they are legally authorized to do so in their state of residence. Some states impose limitations on the authority of nonresident ministers to perform marriages. Before agreeing to perform a marriage in another state, check with civil authorities in that state to be sure you are authorized to perform the marriage.

What are the legal requirements for a valid marriage?

Every state has enacted legislation prescribing various requirements that must be satisfied in order for a lawful marriage to occur. While there is much variation among the states, some requirements are common. These include the following:

What Legal Requirements Apply to the Performance of Marriage Ceremonies?

Legal capacity. Each state prescribes those persons who are not permitted to marry, or who may marry only if certain conditions are satisfied. For example, persons who are related too closely are prohibited from marrying in all states, although the prohibited degree of relationship varies widely. Also, persons below a specified age are prohibited from marrying without the consent of one or both parents, or a court. Many states prohibit marriages between persons with a mental disability and imprisoned felons. Persons with a living spouse are also barred from marrying. It is important for ministers to become familiar with their state's description of those persons who are authorized, and not authorized, to marry.

License. Most states forbid a minister from performing a marriage unless the couple has obtained a marriage license. In many states, such licenses are obtained from the county recorder's office. Licenses are obtained by completing and submitting an application to the appropriate government office, along with the applicable fee. License applications generally ask for biographical and residential information. Licenses usually are valid for only a specified period of time, and only in the county in which they were issued. Some states require a blood test as a condition to receiving a marriage license. Many states impose a "waiting period" of a few days after an application for a license has been submitted until the license may be issued. Ministers may be criminally liable for marrying couples with expired licenses. Well in advance of a marriage, the minister should request a copy of the marriage license, and ensure that it does not expire prior to the wedding date.

Ministers should be familiar with the license requirements under local law, and share this information with engaged couples. Many counties publish pamphlets for engaged couples that summarize the license requirements. It would be a good practice for ministers to have a supply of these publications on hand.

The ceremony. State laws provide little guidance with regard to the content of the marriage ceremony itself. Most statutes simply state that ministers may perform marriages in accordance with their religious tradition and tenets.

The marriage certificate. Most states require ministers to complete a marriage certificate after the solemnization of a marriage, and return it to the same government office that issues marriage licenses. A second certificate often is obtained, and is given to the married couple. State law generally prescribes the deadline for filing marriage certificates, and the penalty for not doing so. Misspelling a name, inserting the wrong date, or having less than the required number of witness signatures on the marriage certificate will not affect the validity of the marriage. It is generally held that a marriage will be considered valid even though the minister fails to complete and return a marriage certificate. And, a marriage will be valid even though the minister performing the ceremony was not authorized to do so, at least if the parties did not know that the minister lacked authority.

Criminal penalties. Many states impose criminal penalties upon ministers for the following acts: (1) failure to maintain a record of marriage ceremonies performed; (2) failure to return promptly to the proper authorities a properly completed certificate of marriage and the license to marry; (3) marrying persons without a marriage license, or with an expired license; (4) marrying persons not legally capable of marrying (because of age, relationship, or some other disability specified by state law).

Pre-marriage legal checklist

Here is a checklist of items to consider before performing a marriage:

- Am I legally qualified to perform a marriage according to the law of my state? Review your state's law. If in doubt, contact your local recorder's office or the office of the attorney general for an interpretation.

- Am I legally qualified to perform a marriage according to the law of another state? Ministers occasionally are asked to perform a marriage in another state. Review the other state's law. If in doubt, contact the recorder's office in the county where the marriage will occur, or the office of the attorney general in the other state.

- Is the engaged couple legally capable of marrying? You will need to check your state law for the legal qualifications for marriage. Every state lists certain conditions that will limit a person's legal right to marry, or even prohibit it. Common examples include persons who are below a specified age, or persons who are too closely related. During premarital counseling be sure to verify that the couple meets all of the eligibility requirements specified by your state's law.

- Be sure you explain to the couple the marriage license requirements prescribed by state law. Again, you need to be familiar with these. They can be obtained from your county recorder's office or the office of your state attorney general.

- Be sure that the couple has a valid marriage license with an expiration date later than the date of the marriage. Check the license several days or weeks prior to the wedding.

- Be sure that the marriage license is valid for the county in which the marriage will occur. Generally, a marriage license is valid only if the marriage occurs in the county in which the license was issued.

- Be sure you make a record of each marriage that you perform, in the manner prescribed by your state law.

- Be sure to complete a certificate of marriage (if required by state law), and return it to the appropriate government office.

"Religious marriages"

Pastors occasionally are called upon by parishioners to perform a "religious" marriage ceremony without complying with the legal requirements for a valid marriage prescribed by state law. There are many reasons for doing so. Consider the following examples:

- One or both spouses is an undocumented alien.

- Compliance with one or more of the civil law requirements is not possible. For example, a couple failed to obtain a license within the time prescribed by law, or one of the spouses is underage.

- A pastor is asked to perform a marriage in another state in which nonresident pastors are not authorized to perform marriages.

- A divorced spouse will lose alimony from her former husband if she remarries.

- A divorced spouse will lose insurance or other benefits in the event of remarriage.

- A couple believes that their Social Security retirement benefits will be higher if they are not legally married.

- A couple regards the civil law requirements for marriage as an unnecessary nuisance, or even an unwarranted government intrusion into an essentially religious ceremony.

Whatever the reason, pastors should understand that there are several potential legal and tax consequences associated with a "religious" marriage that is not in compliance with state law, including those listed below. Pastors may be subject to criminal penalties (typically a misdemeanor involving a fine or short prison sentence) under state law for performing a marriage that does not comply with state law. It is imperative for pastors to understand the possible application of such penalties before performing a religious marriage.

- A religious marriage that does not comply with civil law requirements may preclude one spouse from suing for money damages based on "loss of consortium" for injuries sustained by the other.

- In general, your tax filing status depends on whether you are considered unmarried or married. You are considered unmarried for the whole year if, on the last day of your tax year, you are unmarried. State law governs whether you are married or legally separated under a divorce or separate maintenance decree. An unmarried couple may not file a joint tax return as a married couple. Each files an individual tax return.

- If a couple is "considered married" for the whole year they can file a joint return, or separate returns. A couple is "considered married" for the whole year if on the last day of the tax year they were living together in a common law marriage recognized in the state where they live or in the state where the common law marriage began. Only nine states currently recognize common law marriages, and in many of these states only some common law marriages are recognized.

What Legal Requirements Apply to the Performance of Marriage Ceremonies?

- An unmarried person may be able to file as head of household if certain conditions are met

- An unmarried couple cannot claim each other as an exemption on their individual tax returns.

- An unmarried couple can claim each other as a dependent on their individual tax returns, unless certain conditions are met.

- Unmarried persons cannot combine tax deductions, and cannot claim expenses paid by their partner.

- The phaseout for an IRA deduction begins at a lower amount of income for unmarried persons than for married persons.

- Married spouses generally avoid estate taxes upon the death of the first spouse. This is not necessarily the case with unmarried partners.

- Married spouses generally can transfer property back and forth without gift taxes due to the unlimited marital deduction. This is not the case with unmarried partners.

- If an employer provides health benefits to employees and their "domestic partners," the amount paid by the employer is generally a tax-free fringe benefit to employees but is taxable to unmarried partners.

- An unmarried partner generally cannot receive death benefits payable as a result of the death of the other partner. There is an exception for couples who have a "common law marriage" recognized under state law. However, these marriages are recognized in only nine states, and conditions apply.

- Unmarried partners can execute wills (or other legally enforceable instruments) that leave some or all of their estate to a surviving partner. However, without a will, a deceased partner's estate that is not otherwise disposed of will be distributed according to the law of intestacy. Unmarried partners have no rights under intestacy laws. A few states have passed laws that permit domestic partners to receive a share of a deceased partner's estate.

- If an unmarried couple ends their relationship, there generally is no right of alimony or support from one former partner to the other. A few states have enacted legislation that in some circumstances permits the provision of support (sometimes called "palimony") from one former partner to the other. Conditions apply.

Pastors should not consider performing such a ceremony without carefully considering these possible ramifications. Legal counsel can assist pastors in making an informed decision.

QUIZ ANSWER KEY
1-C, 2-C, 3-B, 4-D

Resources

Online Resources

ChurchLawAndTax.com provides comprehensive, searchable, and easily-accessible information on legal, tax, financial, and risk management matters affecting churches and clergy. The full archives of both *Church Law & Tax Report* and *Church Finance Today* reside on the site as does the Richard R. Hammar Legal Library.

Books and Other Resources

ChurchLawAndTaxStore.com

Church & Clergy Tax Guide

Find comprehensive help understanding United States tax laws as they relate to pastors and churches with Richard Hammar's annual *Church & Clergy Tax Guide*. Tax law in general is highly complex and ever changing. Add to that the many unique rules that apply to church and clergy and you're set up for a challenging task that requires an expert's guidance.

Church Finance: The Complete Guide to Managing Ministry Resources

Overseeing the financial health of a church is no simple task. Increased regulations, IRS audits, and changing technology are a few of the challenges facing both new and experienced treasurers, bookkeepers, business administrators, and executive pastors. *Church Finance*, the groundbreaking comprehensive guide created by respected expert and CPA, Michael E. Batts gives you the confidence you need to manage every aspect of your job.

Made in the USA
Columbia, SC
29 July 2021